Haikuing the Camino
By Robert Mutlow

Illustrations by Amor Coetzee

For Pauline

Introduction

As my 60th birthday approached in 2012 I began to think about walking the Famous Pilgrimage Camino de Santiago to celebrate life and the milestone that was coming up on June 2.
I did not wish to take a camera or phone with me as I desired the experience to be as authentic as possible. I wished to immerse myself in the atmosphere of the pilgrimage and to be open to whatever arose.

My wife Pauline made the brilliant suggestion that I write a Haiku everyday and send it to her by sms. In this way she would know that I was okay and she would be able to follow my journey. I recorded every day of my pilgrimage by writing a Haiku, which I have now collated into this book.

I was fortunate when in 2015 Pauline introduced me to a talented artist Amor Coetzee. Having seen some of her work I approached Amor and asked her if she would be interested in doing some clean, minimalist illustrations depicting my Haikus graphically.
Amor understood exactly what I wanted to express. Her illustrations tell the story of my pilgrimage with such clarity and simplicity. It's as if she herself had walked the Camino.

- Robert Mutlow

Haze in yellow light
Blue Mountains fill the Horizon
Steel Birds waiting

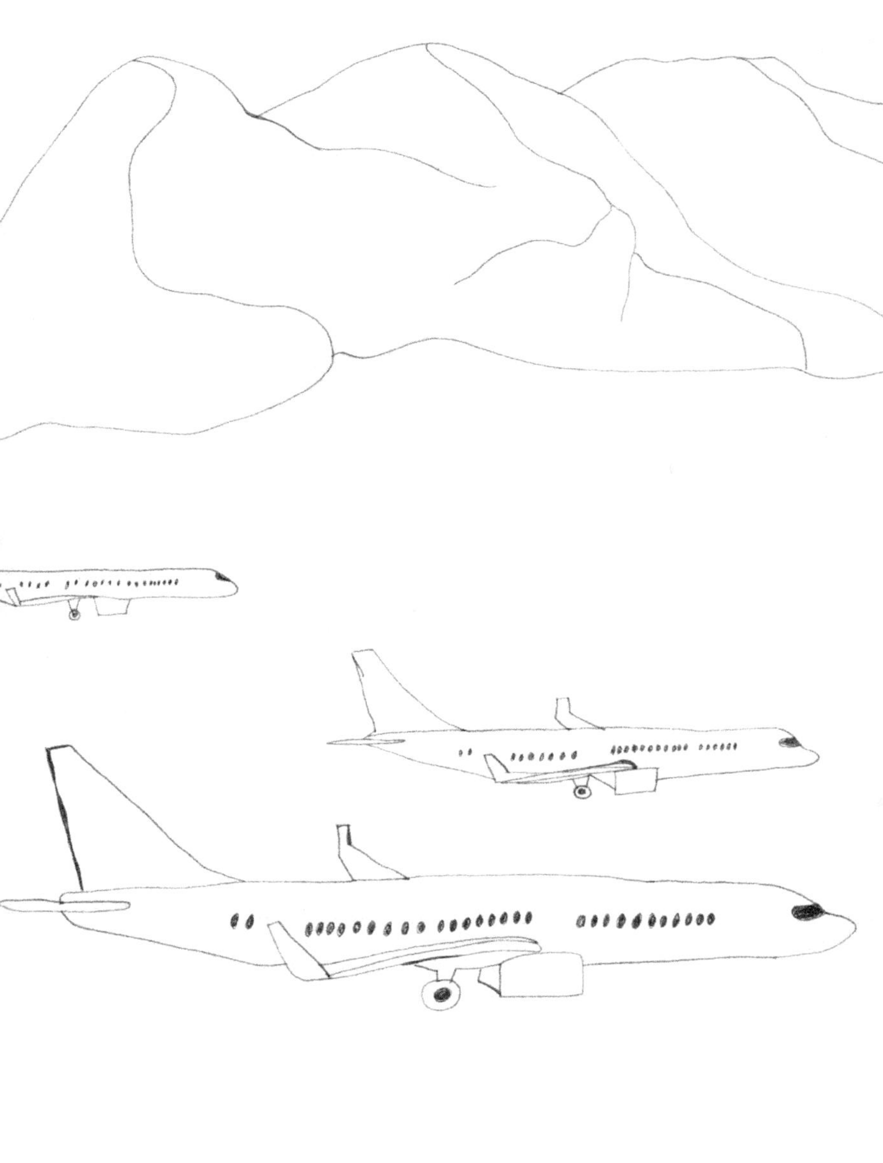

Grey to green
Trees meeting the new season
River moving swiftly

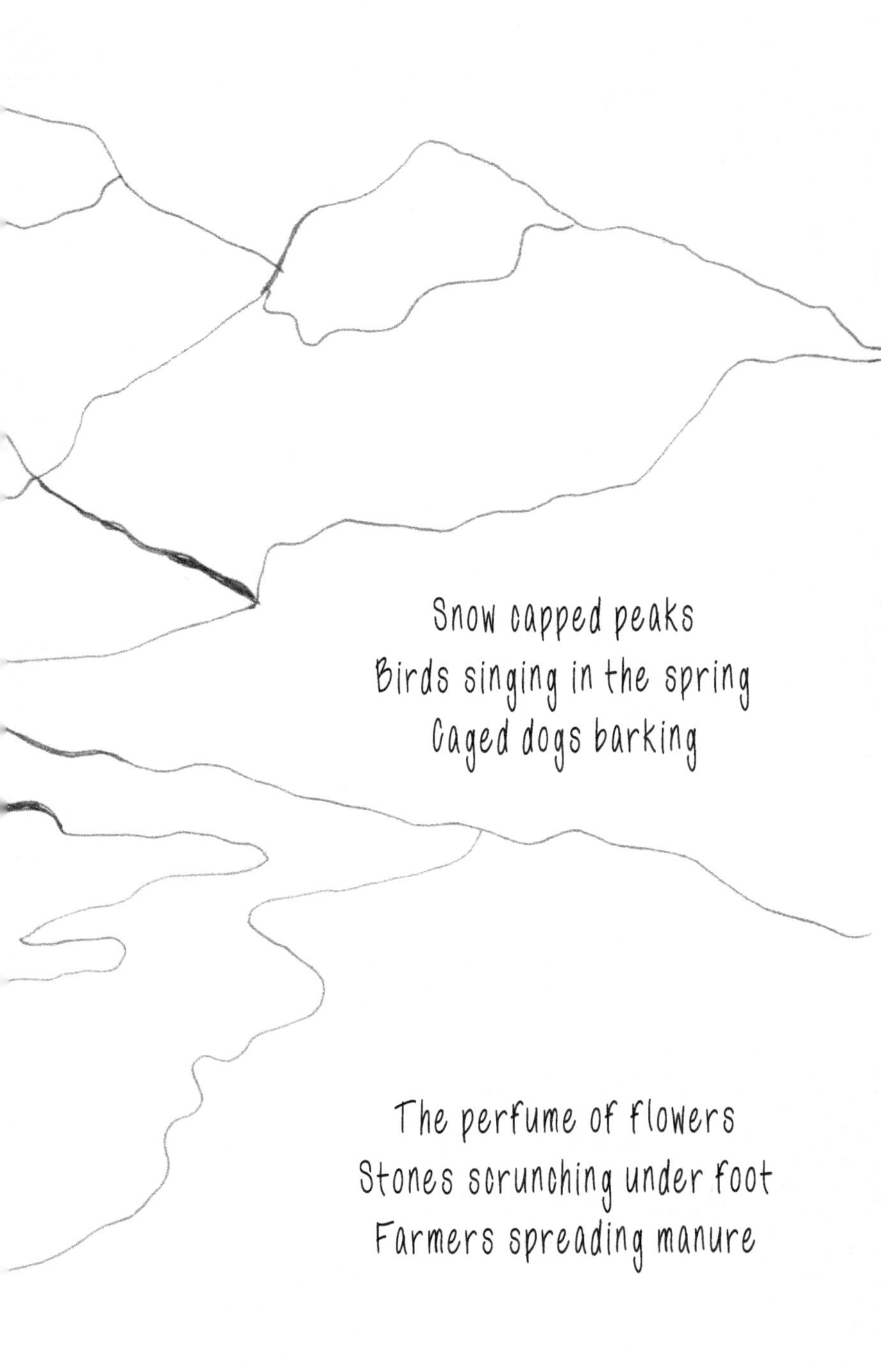
Snow capped peaks
Birds singing in the spring
Caged dogs barking

The perfume of flowers
Stones scrunching under foot
Farmers spreading manure

Rolling green fields
Beautiful handmade dry stonewalls
Electricity cable overhead

Quiet country lanes
Farms rising up with the spring
Aristocrat rides by

Green leaves on the trees
Brown leaves cover the ground
White tissue everywhere

Soft green fields
Fat puffy bursting rolling hills
Trucks roaring past

Soldiers on maneuvers
Automatic gunfire echoes across the valley
Poppies all around

Turbines in the wind
Atop the mountains like tombstones
To a generation of excess

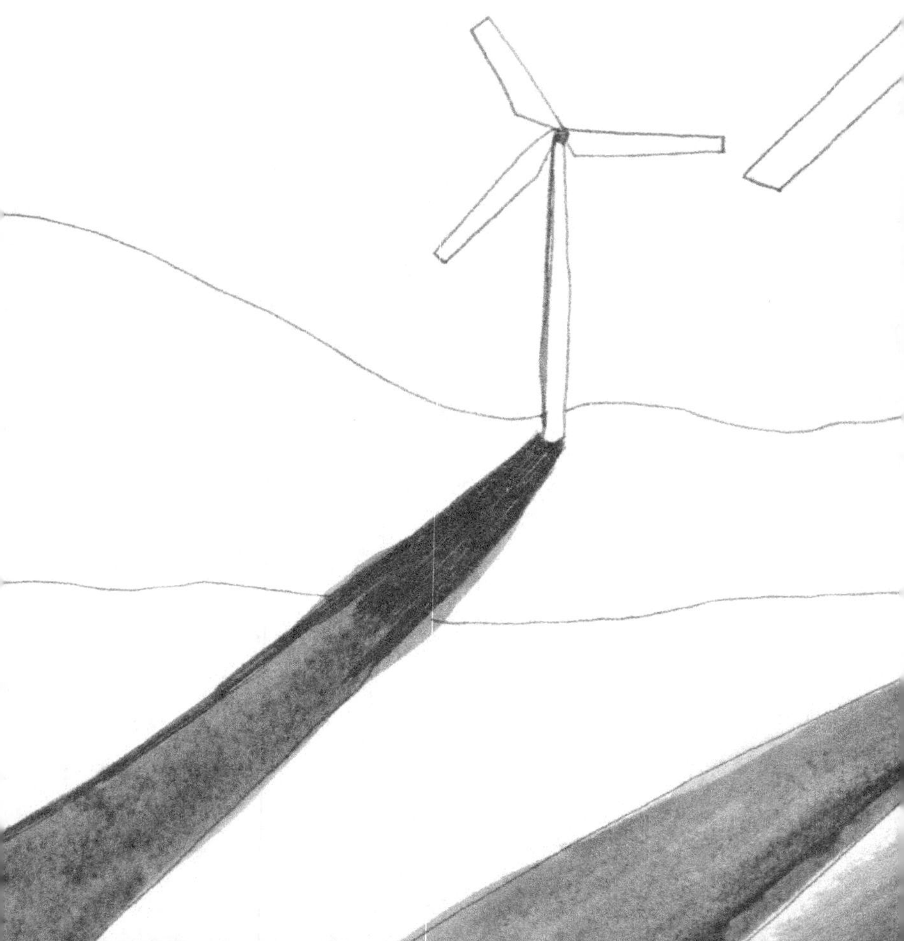

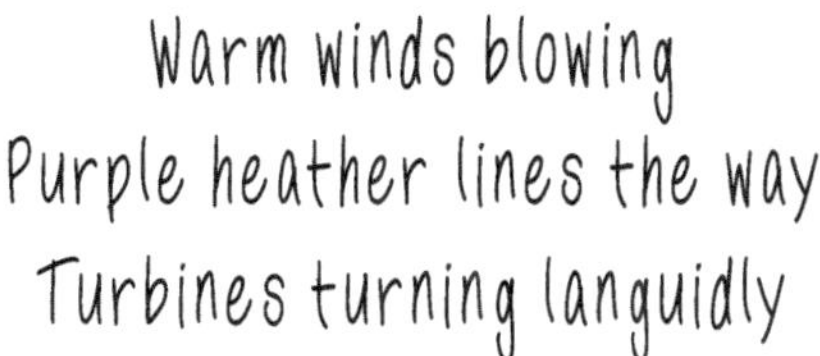

Warm winds blowing
Purple heather lines the way
Turbines turning languidly

I stand upright
Brown smudge on the soil
I am alive

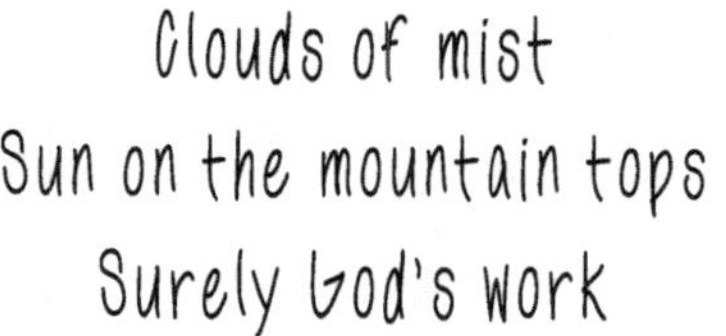

Clouds of mist
Sun on the mountain tops
Surely God's work

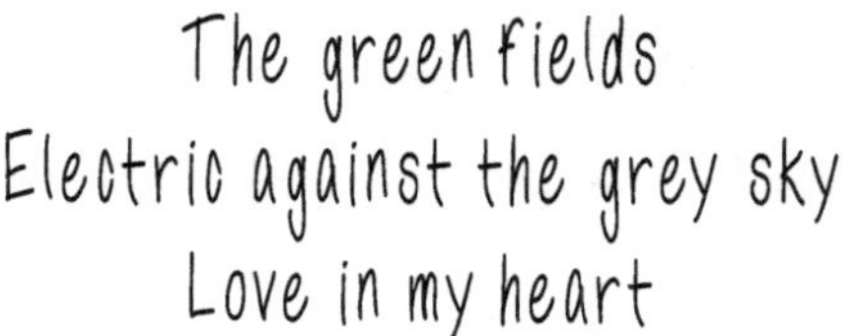

The green fields
Electric against the grey sky
Love in my heart

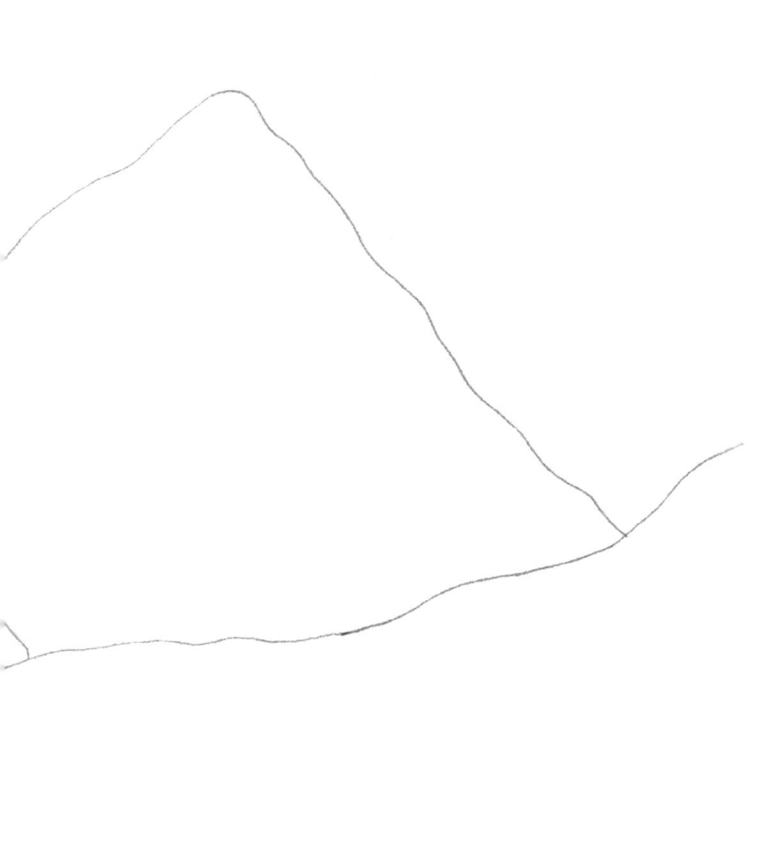

Your understanding
Of what is love
Is truly amazing

Wind cleans my head
Rain water washes my soul
Only love remains

Full of confidence
Full of ego I was humbled
By the Camino

An ancient bridge
Hot air balloons in the sky
What has changed

Snow on the mountains
Cuckoo in the woods, Oh!
To be alive

The sun rising
Flashes of red across the sky
Breath like mist

Birds singing happily
Boots crunching on the earth
What more desired

Sun on my back
A shadow on the path ahead
That's all I am

Sun breaks through
Strange shadows from my rain cape
Is this I

Birds flying by
Jet streams in the sky
God versus Man

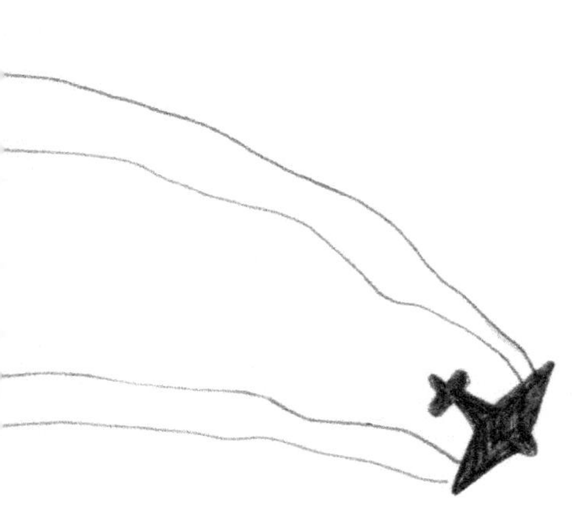

Grey black sky
Rainbow stretching from the horizon
All is good

Clear water rushing
Green moss bending in the current
Bit like humanity

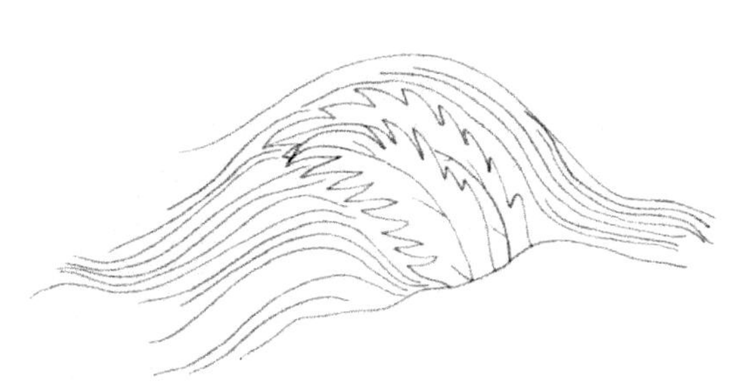

Life death fear
All one of the same
Scared of living

I never realized
Rubbing cream on my toes
So much love

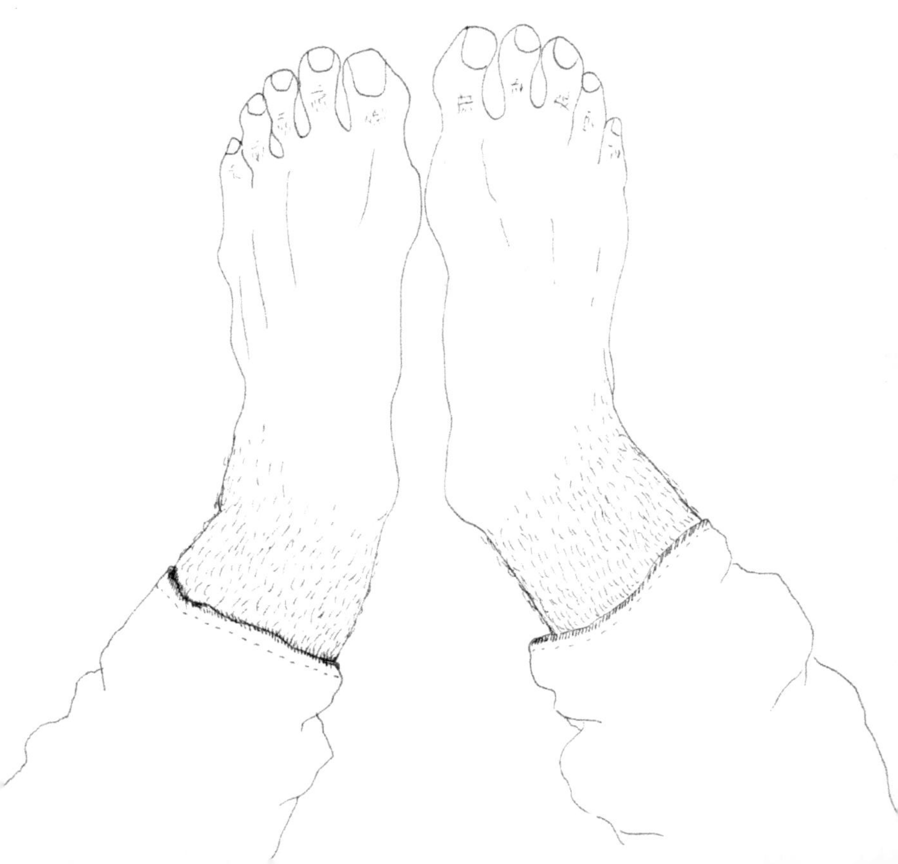

I smell you
When I open my little book
My heart leaps

Straight road ahead
My thoughts wander to you
How, I love you

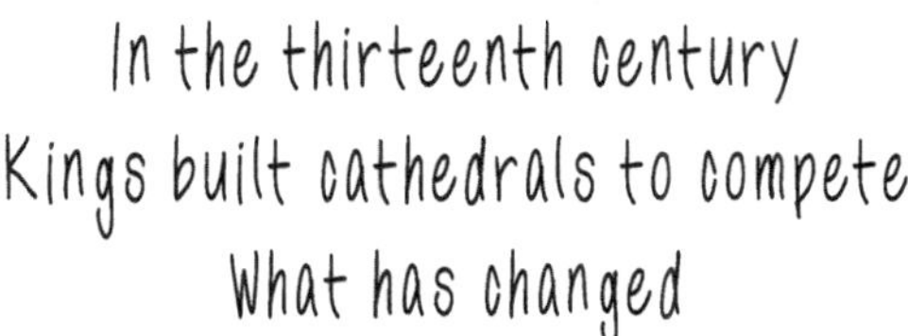

In the thirteenth century
Kings built cathedrals to compete
What has changed

Soft milky sky
Smell of flowers intoxicating
Industry in sight

Dirty defaced city
Manicured suburbs, soulless houses
Hardworking country peasants

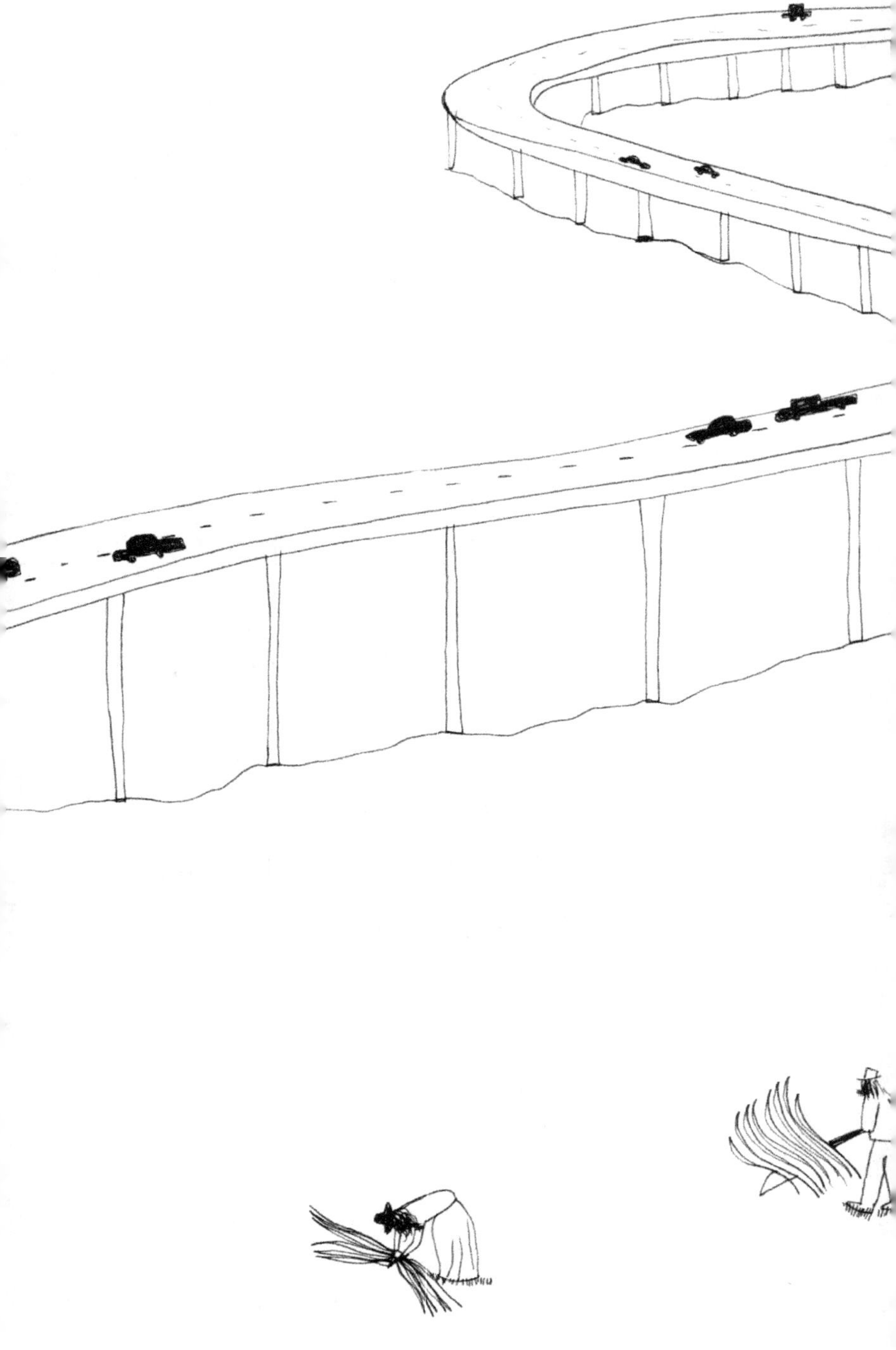

Pilgrims in the valley
Highway like monorails in the sky
Peasants working their land

Fat monks about
Given their lives to God
Or, given up

Walking this morning
The mist surrounds me, as love
Embraced by you

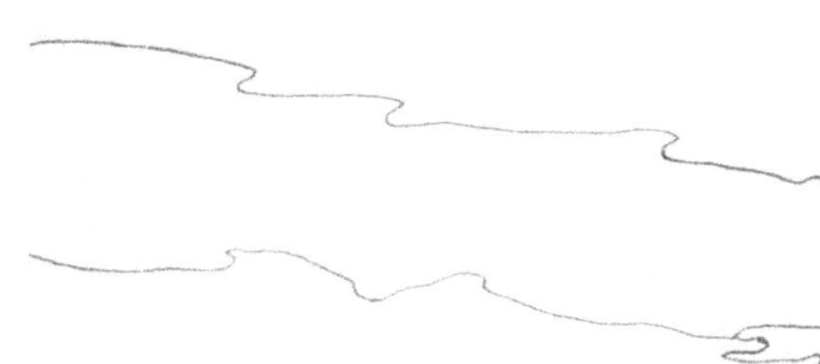

A beautiful voice
Such lovely gentle hand movements
Disinterested deaf humanity

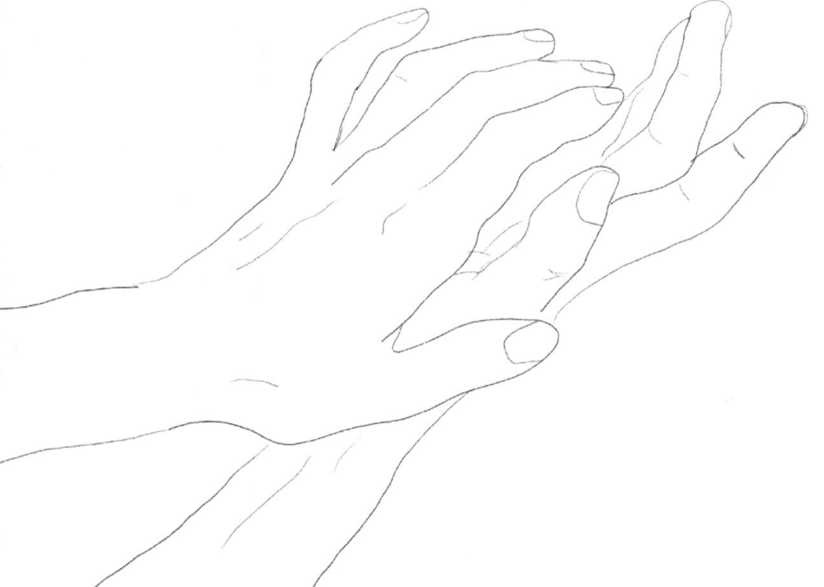

Sun on the sea
What the Camino meant to me
Walking with God

Sea alongside road
Longing to be home again
A changed man

Tired but alive
I understand love in this state
Will it endure

My heart open
I have reached the conclusion
Love is the way

To arrive home
Into your loving arms again
This is life

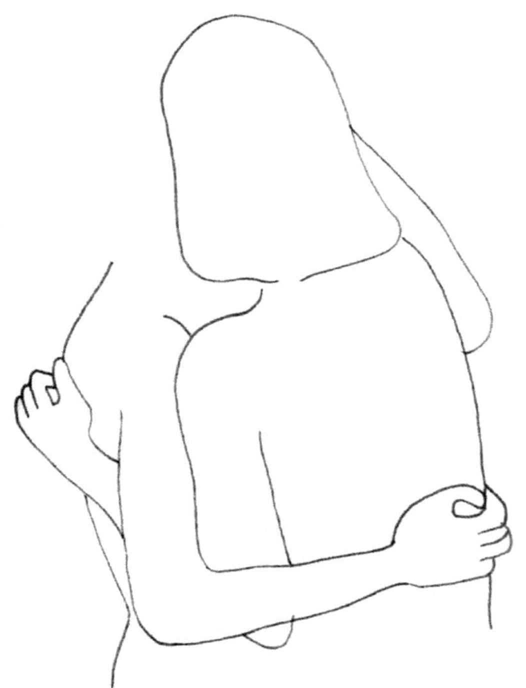